BEYOND THE CLASSROOM

READING AND WRITING IN YOUR LIFE

by Charis Mather

BEARPORT PUBLISHING

Fusion Books, an imprint of Bearport Publishing by FlutterBee

Credits
All images are courtesy of Shutterstock.com, unless otherwise specified. With thanks to Getty Images, Thinkstock Photo, and iStockphoto. Cover, © Ground Picture, Kate Krasovskaya, Line By Line Vectors, Lima das Artes, Miljan Zivkovic, PreciousJ, Colorfuel Studio, Eram Design, Rolling Stones, AlyonaZhitnaya, Yganko, Kobee, Nikolai V Titov. Throughout, © Line By Line Vectors, NM-art; 4–5, © PR Image Factory, igor kisselev; 6–7, © Monkey Business Images, Ground Picture; 8–9, © Jorge Aguado Martin/iStockphoto, kool99/iStockphoto; 10–11, © GaudiLab, VP Photo Studio, wellphoto, VGstockstudio, Pressmaster; 12–13, © wavebreakmedia, kenchiro168; 14–15, © Ground Picture, Littlekidmoment, Random Illustrator, GoodStudio; 16–17, © Monkey Business Images, New Africa; 18–19, © LightField Studios, Tero Vesalainen, New Vectors; 20–21, © Irina WS, Evgeny Atamanenko; 22–23, © Ermolaev Alexander, Pressmaster.

Bearport Publishing Company Product Development Team
Kayla Eggert, Theresa Emminizer, Kim Jones, Allison Juda, Cole Nelson, Naomi Reich, Steve Scheluchin, Tiana Tran

Library of Congress Cataloging-in-Publication Data is available at www.loc.gov or upon request from the publisher.

ISBN: 979-8-89577-609-4 (hardcover)
ISBN: 979-8-89577-697-1 (ebook)

For more information, write to Bearport Publishing, 3500 American Blvd W, Suite 150, Bloomington, MN 55431.
Printed in the United States of America.

CONTENTS

ALL ABOUT READING AND WRITING

Have you ever wondered . . .

. . . why do I need to learn to read and write?

If you have ever felt that way, you might be surprised. Reading and writing are more than school subjects. They are key life skills.

Think about it. You use them every day! You read street signs, labels, books, and much more. You write to **communicate** information or to share your ideas with others.

WHY IT MATTERS

Besides talking, reading and writing are the main ways people communicate. If you don't know how to read, you'll find it hard to understand what's going on around you.

Reading and writing are some of the first things we learn in school. That is because once we know how to read, we can learn about almost anything!

WIDEN YOUR WORLD

Reading lets you learn about far-off places you have never seen before. It helps you imagine what it's like to live a life that is different from your own.

Reading can help you build **empathy**. When you read stories, see what **characters** are thinking. You can feel what it's like to be them.

The books you read can open your mind to new ideas.

COOL CAREERS

There are many exciting **careers** for people with strong reading and writing skills.

Lawyers read about old cases to help them follow the law.

Authors write books.

Journalists write about important world events.

World leaders need to communicate clearly.

Screenwriters write movies and TV shows.

Being able to read and write is part of almost every job.

BOOKS FOR YOU

There are lots of different kinds of books. Nonfiction books are about real people and events. Reading nonfiction is a great way to learn about things you are interested in.

What kind of books do you like to read?

Made-up stories are called fiction. Reading fiction is fun! Some books are about imaginary worlds, people, and adventures. Some books are about kids just like you!

Looking for books? Try your local library!

WRITING FOR FUN

If you have a big imagination and lots of interesting ideas, creative writing is a great way to express yourself! Some people make up stories to share with others. But there are other ways to write for fun, too.

Do you like to write stories?

Try coming up with a new ending to your favorite story. Or take turns writing parts of a story with a friend. You could write a song to sing. Maybe you could even write and draw your own comic book!

Writing in a diary can be just for you. It can help you work through big feelings.

KEEPING TRACK OF INFORMATION

When you have information that you do not want to forget, being able to write it down is very important. Many students write notes to help them remember what their lessons were about.

Writing notes is also useful outside of the classroom. You could write shopping lists or reminders of things you want to buy or do. Some people write events on a calendar.

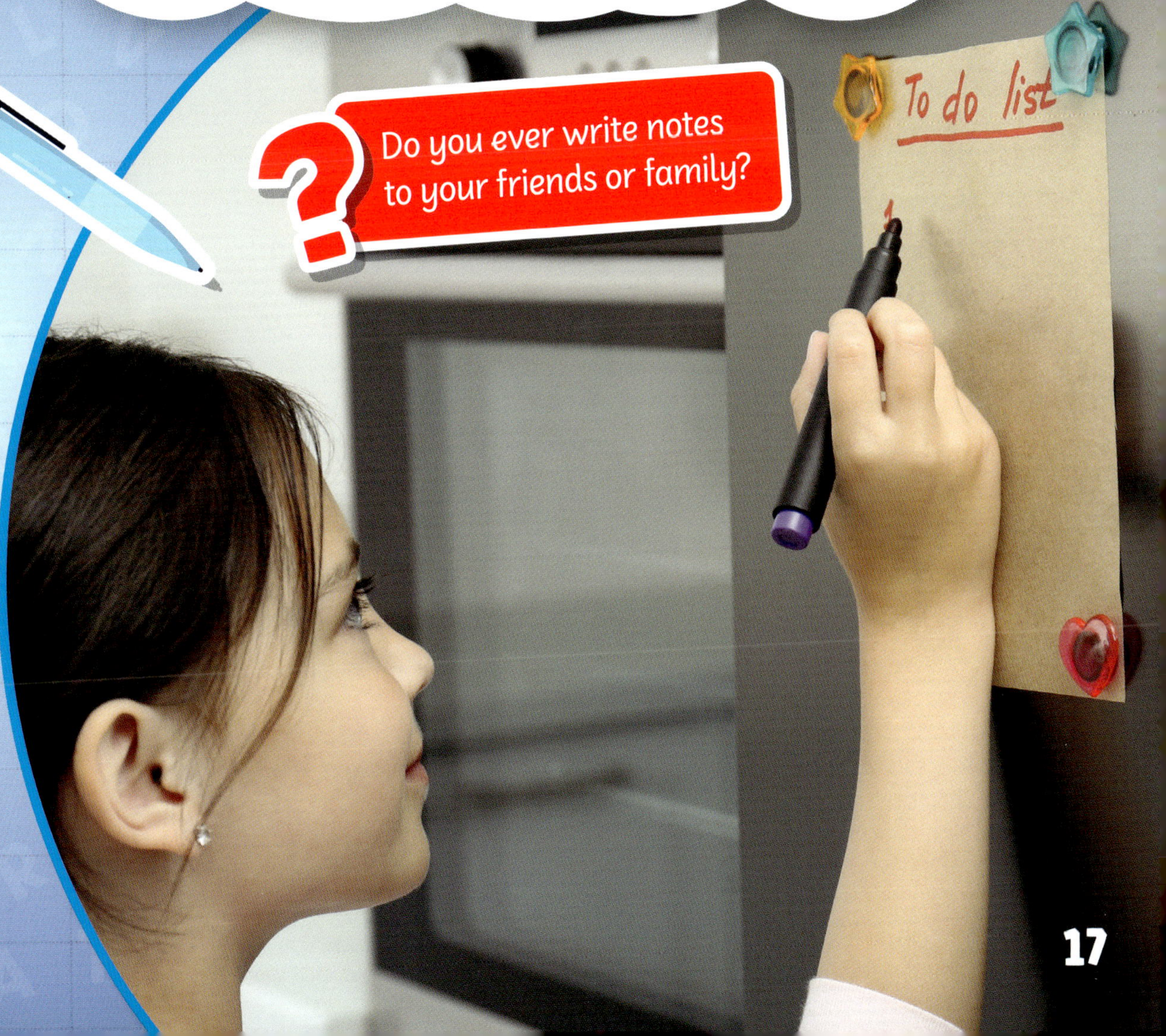

Do you ever write notes to your friends or family?

KEEPING UP WITH THE WORLD

Reading the news can help you keep up with what is going on in the world. But it's important to think carefully about what you are reading. Not everything you read is true.

Ask a trusted grown-up to help you find good **sources** of information. You can fact-check what you read by comparing the info from a few different sources.

Finding trustworthy sources online can be tricky. Sites that end in .edu or .gov are usually **reliable**.

STAYING CONNECTED

Reading and writing help us connect with others. If someone you love lives far away, you can write them a letter.

Writing a card or a letter is a great way to celebrate special events. You could write a birthday card or send someone a note to tell them you are thinking of them.

You can write an email or text to get in touch with someone quickly.

PRACTICING WHAT YOU KNOW

Reading and writing are powerful tools that help us learn about the world and connect with others. We use these tools every day!

There are so many fun ways to read and write outside the classroom. Write a play and perform it with friends! Read a book and draw the characters. Let your imagination grow!

How will you practice reading and writing today?

GLOSSARY

careers jobs that people have for a long time

characters people from stories

communicate to pass information between two or more people

empathy being able to understand how someone else is feeling

reliable able to be trusted

sources places to find information about something

INDEX